LET'S GET INTO S.H.A.P.E. SPREADING HAPPINESS ACROSS PLANET EARTH

52 HAPPY Hints To Turn Your Frown Upside Down

Amanda Lindsey
Spreader of the HAPPY

Divine Destiny Publishing

Copyright © 2025 Amanda Lindsey and Divine Destiny Publishing

All Rights Reserved. Apart from any fair dealing for the purposes of research or private study, or criticism or review, as permitted under the Copyright, Designs and Patents Act 1988, this publication may only be reproduced, stored or transmitted, in any form or by any means, with the prior permission in writing of the copyright owner, or in the case of the reprographic reproduction in accordance with the terms of licensees issued by the Copyright Licensing Agency. Inquiries concerning reproduction outside those terms should be sent to the publisher.

Let's Get Into S.H.A.P.E.

Spreading Happiness Across Planet Earth

It's A Happiness Revolution!!

CONTENTS

Title Page
Copyright
Introduction … 1
Part 1: Cultivating Your Inner HAPPY … 7
HAPPY Hint #1: Get Curious About Your Own Happiness … 9
HAPPY Hint #2: Smile At Your Reflection AND Whenever You See Or Hear Your Name … 12
HAPPY Hint #3: Create A HAPPY Box … 15
HAPPY Hint #4: Turn Your Have-To's Into Get-To's … 18
HAPPY Hint #5: Cuddle A Critter--Live or Stuffed Animal … 21
HAPPY Hint #6: Sing, Whistle, Or Hum A HAPPY Tune … 24
HAPPY Hint #7: Transform The Ordinary Into The Extraordinary … 28
HAPPY Hint #8: Move Your Body … 32
HAPPY Hint #9: Keep Your Eyes On The HAPPY Prize … 35
HAPPY Hint #10: Stop And Smell The HAPPY … 39
HAPPY Hint #11: Hear And/Or Feel The HAPPY Vibes … 43
HAPPY Hint #12: Throw A Party For Your Palate … 46
HAPPY Hint #13: Honor Your Awesomeness … 49
HAPPY Hint #14: Venture Outside … 52
HAPPY Hint #15: Rest, Relax, Renew, Receive … 55

HAPPY Hint #16: Create A Positivity Word Bank	58
HAPPY Hint #17: Give Yourself A Love Note Or Letter	62
HAPPY Hint #18: Let Your Inner Artist Shine	67
HAPPY Hint #19: Dream Big	71
HAPPY Hint #20: Schedule a Happiness Check-in	75
HAPPY Hint #21: BE Present	80
HAPPY Hint #22: Literally Laugh Out Loud	84
HAPPY Hint #23: Play	88
HAPPY Hint #24: Try Something New	92
HAPPY Hint #25: Pause, Breathe, Appreciate	96
HAPPY Hint #26: Choose Joy For Yourself	100
Part 2: Sharing Your HAPPY	103
HAPPY Hint #1: Get Curious About The Happiness Of Those Around You	105
HAPPY Hint #2: Give A Gracious Greeting	108
HAPPY Hint #3: Nurture With Nature	112
HAPPY Hint #4: Send Some Snail Mail	116
HAPPY Hint #5: Start A Meaningful Conversation	119
HAPPY Hint #6: Congratulate Someone On A Job Well Done	123
HAPPY Hint #7: Participate In Local HAPPY	127
HAPPY Hint #8: Participate In Global HAPPY	130
HAPPY Hint #9: Open A Door For Someone	133
HAPPY Hint #10: Pay A Genuine Compliment	137
HAPPY Hint #11: Take Or Be Part Of A Group Photo	141
HAPPY Hint #12: Phone A Friend Or Loved One	145
HAPPY Hint #13: Recall, Remember, Reminisce	148
HAPPY Hint #14: Create A New Shared Tradition	152
HAPPY Hint #15: Actively Listen	155

HAPPY Hint #16: Mix And Mingle	158
HAPPY Hint #17: Reach Out And Touch Someone	161
HAPPY Hint #18: Marinate In A Magical Moment Of Silence	164
HAPPY Hint #19: Revel In Random Acts Of Happiness	167
HAPPY Hint#20: Tell A Funny Joke Or Story	170
HAPPY Hint #21: Acknowledge And Say Thank You	173
HAPPY Hint #22: Give And Receive The Gift Of Assistance	177
HAPPY Hint #23: Savor The Flavor	181
HAPPY Hint #24: Pay It Forward	185
HAPPY Hint #25: Organize An Outing	188
HAPPY HinT #26: Choose Joy With Others	192
Part 3: Bonus HAPPY	195
HAPPY Hint #53:	197
Sources	199
About The Author	201
	203

INTRODUCTION

As *Spreader of the HAPPY*, I believe that deep down we all want the most happiness possible in our lives and the lives of others...or at least we *want* to want these things. However, at times, I know that this idea may seem ridiculous and downright impossible—trust me, I've been there.

After twelve horrendous years of dealing with daily, debilitating chronic health issues, I had lost a genuine connection to myself and others. Barely able to move due to severe joint pain and extreme exhaustion, I became jobless, went through a divorce, and lost friends left and right—I felt I had hit rock bottom. And if that wasn't bad enough, around this time, the

COVID-19 pandemic decided to rear its ugly head.

Curiously enough, these troublesome times brought about what I call my *Happiness Awakening*. Somehow, with a HAPPY and Grateful heart, I experienced a reconnection with myself and the rest of humanity. Unfortunately, this awakening came from witnessing the harsh similarities between my chronic health issues and the struggles of billions of people worldwide—who were simultaneously undergoing a complete upheaval of their normal lives. Fear of the unknown, along with overwhelming feelings of anger, isolation, confusion, and stress—combined with limited mobility and financial instability—became a daily reality.

I realized that no matter who we were as individuals, where we lived on the planet, or what our unique experiences had been, we could all be linked through pain and suffering.

This bittersweet realization was intolerable. I longed for an entirely new connection with the world—one built on Happiness, Hope, Laughter, Love, and Positivity. This burning desire gave rise to my mission: *Getting into S.H.A.P.E. (Spreading Happiness Across Planet Earth)*.

What is Getting into S.H.A.P.E.?

Getting into S.H.A.P.E. is a Happiness Revolution!

It's a magical adventure that involves *Cultivating The*

Happiness Within and Then Sharing It With Others. First and foremost, it's about creating and fostering a loving connection with yourself—discovering what truly brings you joy. The happiness journey ultimately begins with you. As I like to say, *A Happier Me makes a Happier We.*

Getting into S.H.A.P.E. is also a powerful decision, one that only you can make. You alone possess the happiness superpowers of choice and responsibility. You decide what lights a *HAPPY Fire* within your belly. You choose how and when to show up to fan the flames.

Finally, *Getting into S.H.A.P.E.* is a practice, much like getting into physical shape. The more you use your *HAPPY Muscles,* the more they grow and evolve. The more connected you become to your joy, the more joyful your life becomes. And as your life becomes more joyful, you'll naturally want to spread that happiness to others—encouraging and inspiring them to do the same.

How do you Get into S.H.A.P.E?

The happiness revolution begins by embracing and honoring the *Five C's of Getting into S.H.A.P.E.*—Curiosity, Connection, Cooperation, Collaboration, and Celebration. These Five C's first allow you to go inward to cultivate and create your own happiness. Then, they allow you to spread it like wildfire.

- **Curiosity and Connection** bring Awareness and Acknowledgment—both of yourself and others—when it comes to happiness. The more you ask questions about your own joy, desires, and goals, the more connected you become to yourself. Likewise, getting curious about the joy, desires, and goals of others deepens your connection with them.

- **Cooperation and Collaboration** involve Inspired Action. It's about working toward the joy, desires, and goals you've discovered—both for yourself and for those around you. Cooperation focuses on individual goals, while collaboration revolves around shared joy, desires, and goals.

- **Celebration** is all about Gratitude and Appreciation. It's the moment to acknowledge every win, no matter how big or small, on your journey toward happiness. Celebration is crucial because it allows you to truly receive the fruits of your labor—and it's the ultimate motivator for continuing to pursue your HAPPY and share it with others.

When it comes to *Getting into S.H.A.P.E.*, the possibilities are endless! Each roadmap is as beautifully unique as the person behind the wheel. In this book, I've compiled **52 HAPPY Hints** to help get you started on your journey. May these HAPPY Hints activate the

Five C's of Getting into S.H.A.P.E. and turn your frowns upside down!

Organization of the Book

- **Part 1 presents 26 ideas to Get Yourself into S.H.A.P.E.** The happiness journey truly begins within, so my first focus is to offer some HAPPY Hints to bring more joy into your world.

- **Part 2 provides 26 suggestions for bringing happiness to others**. Once you've discovered ways to create joy in your own life, it's time to spread those smiles for miles! After all, happiness is even better when shared.

After each HAPPY Hint, you'll find a reflection page titled HAPPY Thoughts—a space for you to document your *Getting into S.H.A.P.E.* journey. Feel free to write directly on the page, print extra copies if you need more space, or save them for future use.

Consider reflecting on questions such as:
- How did you feel before reading about and trying each HAPPY Hint?
- How did you feel afterward?
- Did you experience any "aha moments"?

But remember, this is your happiness adventure—make it

your own!

AND FINALLY A HAPPY SURPRISE…

- **Part 3 reveals a bonus HAPPY Hint!** May it bring joy to *both* you and those around you.

How to Enjoy These HAPPY Hints

I've crafted this happiness experience so that you can focus on one HAPPY Hint per week. You can practice it daily or as often as you like. You can also revisit the book anytime and *Get into S.H.A.P.E.* by randomly selecting HAPPY Hints. There is no right or wrong way to approach this journey—all I ask is that you read with an open heart, mind, and spirit and have fun incorporating these HAPPY Hints into your life.

SO LET THE HAPPINESS REVOLUTION BEGIN, AND LET'S GET INTO S.H.A.P.E.!!

Hugs and Smiles

~ Amanda Lindsey ~

Spreader of the HAPPY

PART 1: CULTIVATING YOUR INNER HAPPY

*26 HAPPY Hints To Bring
More Joy Into Your World*

*Note: If For Some Reason You Are Unable To Enjoy These Happy Hints On Your Own, Ask Someone For Support—The More The Merrier!!

HAPPY HINT #1: GET CURIOUS ABOUT YOUR OWN HAPPINESS

The fun and exciting quest of cultivating your inner happiness begins with curiosity. Curiosity fosters connection through Acknowledgment, Recognition, and Compassion. The more connected you are to yourself, the easier it becomes to be HAPPY.

At what I perceived as the lowest point in my life—physically unable to move, without a job, no friends, and a failed marriage—I finally decided to get curious about my happiness, or rather, my lack of it. I was tired of my pity party and of seeeing myself as nothing more than a numb, motionless lump in bed. The idea of change felt daunting, and my resistance was high, but I pushed myself to start looking inward.

I began asking myself endless questions as if I were getting to know a new friend. I searched for things to love and appreciate about myself, making a conscious effort to be kind and gentle along the way. Journaling on my phone became an easy way to reflect on my thoughts and explore my happiness.

Over time, I started paying closer attention to my surroundings, noticing anything—or anyone—that brought even the slightest smile to my face or a spark of joy to my heart. What once felt like an overwhelming challenge soon became a game—*a happiness game*. And as I grew more curious about my own happiness, I realized something profound: the pursuit of it was what brought me the greatest joy in life.

Now it's your turn to explore!

With this HAPPY Hint, I invite you to discover more about yourself. Get to know YOU and what brings YOU joy. It can be as simple as noticing what makes you smile or as deep as a reflective journaling session. There's no right or wrong way—this is your happiness adventure.

So, go get curious! The more you know about yourself, the more your happiness can grow.

HAPPY Thoughts

HAPPY HINT #2: SMILE AT YOUR REFLECTION AND WHENEVER YOU SEE OR HEAR YOUR NAME

Mirror mirror on the wall, who's the fairest of them all?

It's YOU—and if you don't believe me, I have proof. You, dear one, are not just one in a million—you're one in eight billion, and counting! So, show yourself some love. Flash those pearly whites whenever you pass by a mirror, hear your name spoken aloud, or see it in print.

I love smiling (and making funny faces) at my

reflection first thing when I wake up. It sets a lighthearted, positive tone for the day ahead and gives me an extra pep in my step. I also make it a habit to flash a quick grin at the mirror whenever Nature Calls —a smile while washing my hands goes a long way.

By repeating small actions like these as often as possible, you'll start to associate a smile with things that are uniquely yours. Before long, your reflection and personal identifiers will become symbols of happiness—JUST FOR YOU!

HAPPY Thoughts

HAPPY HINT #3: CREATE A HAPPY BOX

A *HAPPY Box* is a container of treasures that activates or reminds you of your bliss—similar to a keepsake box, but designed for use rather than just storage. Its purpose is to (re)ignite your joy during tough times or enhance your mood when you're already vibing high. Your *HAPPY Box* can be physical or virtual and should always be easily accessible, whether you need a boost or want to amplify your happiness. Having joyful memories readily available to relive sends a powerful signal to your mind, heart, and body that positive, uplifting feelings are what you want to experience.

When creating a physical *HAPPY Box*, I encourage you to make it aesthetically pleasing in a way that reflects your unique style—bright colors, glitter, sparkles, and smiley faces work for me! This not only makes the project fun but also ensures your box catches your attention when you need it most. Once you've designed your *HAPPY Box,* fill it with mementos of good times—and keep adding to it. As your *HAPPY Box* becomes full and heavy with delightful gems of joy, by all means, create another! Personally, I love designing a new *HAPPY Box* every year.

A virtual *HAPPY Box* works much the same way, just without the tactile elements. Create a folder on your phone or any device you use frequently, and fill it with digital keepsakes that make you smile—pictures, emails, texts, video or audio clips, and more. When life feels turbulent, when you need a quick pick-me-up, or even when you just want to savor the joy of the moment, open your virtual *HAPPY Box* and immerse yourself in those cherished treasures.

So, what kinds of magical mementos will you store in your Beloved Box of Bliss?

HAPPY Thoughts

HAPPY HINT #4: TURN YOUR HAVE-TO'S INTO GET-TO'S

You probably make or have made lists before—whether they're daily, weekly, monthly, or even quarterly. You've most likely been conditioned to see these agendas through the lens of I *Have-To*—as in, I *Have-To* complete certain tasks to feel accomplished or to stay employed.

But what if you shifted your perspective to I Get-To?

The idea of *Getting-To* do something puts a more positive spin on any task. It also makes completing it feel more rewarding. Scratching each item off your list brings a deeper sense of accomplishment because you're recognizing it as an opportunity—one that many others may not have.

This shift in mindset has been especially meaningful for me. Take going to the dentist, for example. Years ago, I used to dread *Having-To* go. But then I thought about the days when I was bedridden, unable to voluntarily move anything but my eyes. From that perspective, I would have given anything to *Get-To* go to the dentist.

Saying I *Get-To* also reframes the task as a choice—YOUR choice. Think about it: I *Get-To* go grocery shopping feels far more empowering than I *Have-To* go grocery shopping. When given a choice, your brain and body naturally respond in a more positive way. Choosing to *Get-To* do something allows for more joy than forcing yourself to *Have-To* do it.

And let's be honest—it's just more fun to say: I *Get-To*!

*For an extra dose of fun and happiness—when your responsibilities aren't time-sensitive—turn your *Get-To's* list into a game. Write each task on a strip of paper, fold them up, and place them in a hat, box, or bag. Then pick a random task and complete it!

HAPPY Thoughts

HAPPY HINT #5: CUDDLE A CRITTER--LIVE OR STUFFED ANIMAL

I'm sure you've had a furry pet at some point in your life—or at least a favorite stuffed animal. There's something undeniably soothing about nuzzling soft fur or hugging a beloved companion close. Whether it's a living pet or a cherished stuffed animal, the comfort they provide can instantly lift your spirits.

Studies show that petting a furry friend offers significant health benefits—including lower blood pressure, cholesterol, and triglyceride levels, as well as reduced feelings of loneliness, anxiety, and PTSD symptoms. I can personally attest to these findings. For at my lowest point physically, simply having my cat lying next to me on the bed brought a huge smile to my face and warmth to my heart.

So, whether for comfort, health benefits, or both—go *Cuddle A Critter*. You'll be glad you did!

HAPPY Thoughts

HAPPY HINT #6: SING, WHISTLE, OR HUM A HAPPY TUNE

Have you ever caught yourself randomly singing, whistling, or humming?

If so, chances are you were in a pretty good mood. Just thinking about this HAPPY Hint brings to mind Disney's Snow White and her little forest friends, cheerfully cleaning the house as they sing, "Whistle While You Work." And you better believe each critter has a smile on its face! You, too, are sure to smile as you try this HAPPY Hint.

Singing, *Whistling*, and *Humming* aren't just fun—they also offer wonderful benefits for your body. These simple, joyful activities release endorphins, your body's natural feel-good chemicals. They support heart and lung function by encouraging deep breathing. Plus, they stimulate the vagus nerve, which plays a key role in helping your body relax. *An elevated mood, improved organ function, and a greater sense of calm?* Sounds pretty HAPPY to me!

I can personally attest to the power of this HAPPY Hint—just today, I found myself randomly humming several times, always with a smile on my face. I couldn't tell you why or even what tune I was humming, but I do remember where I was: first, wandering around my house in search of something; next, scanning the aisles at the grocery store for bottled water; and finally, enjoying a walk through my neighborhood. Humming seems to come naturally to me—it requires no effort or thought.

Singing and whistling, on the other hand, are more intentional. I typically sing along to music in the car or during the Happy Birthday song, eagerly awaiting the cake. *And singing karaoke at a bar?* That's definitely on my *Get-To* list!

Whistling, though, is more of a *Try-To* activity for me. I pucker my lips and blow, but the result sounds more like a wind tunnel than a bird song. That doesn't stop me from trying—in fact, it only makes it more fun. I usually end up laughing halfway through!

So, how will you try to embrace this HAPPY Hint?

Maybe you'll sing a lullaby as you tuck your child into bed. Perhaps you'll take Snow White's advice and "whistle while you work." Or, like me, you might not have to try at all—you could just find yourself randomly humming, with a great big smile on your face.

HAPPY Thoughts

HAPPY HINT #7: TRANSFORM THE ORDINARY INTO THE EXTRAORDINARY

Do you ever feel bored with life, like you're just going through the motions day after day?

With this HAPPY Hint, I'll show you how to break free from monotony and shake up the repetitive patterns in your world. Get ready—you're about to embark on a *Happiness Adventure*, transforming the ordinary into the extraordinary!

The real difference between ordinary and

extraordinary is the EXTRA. It's the EXTRA passion you bring to a project. It's the EXTRA joy you find in completing a task. It's the EXTRA creativity, imagination, and magic you infuse into the experience. BEing mindful of this EXTRA—and acting on it—is the secret to turning the mundane into something meaningful.

Take house cleaning, for example. It's never exactly made my heart sing. If you peeked at my *Get-To* list, you'd spot it lounging at the very bottom. *And honestly?* I wouldn't mind if it stayed there. But, for the sake of basic human decency (and the occasional unexpected visitor), it has to be done.

One day, instead of dreading another routine cleaning session, I decided I wasn't going to clean the house —I was going on an important quest. *My mission?* To seek out and rescue all the dust bunnies in my path, including those in hiding. First, I armed myself with the proper weapons to free these captive creatures from my home. Then, I set off on my adventure, searching high and low for every last dust bunny in need of saving.

By choosing to see this ordinary task in an extraordinary light, my entire perception of house cleaning shifted. With a bit of creativity, dust, lint, and hair transformed into tiny critters—dust bunnies (and oh, how they multiply like rabbits!). In my imagination, I became their heroic rescuer, determined to return them to their rightful homes. And as if by magic, I actually started enjoying dusting, sweeping, mopping, and vacuuming.

So, what repetitive, everyday task will you make extraordinary? How will you add your own unique brand of EXTRA to turn it into a glorious adventure?

Whatever you decide, remember this:

EXTRA is what separates the ordinary from the extraordinary—it's the Passion, Joy, Creativity, Imagination, and Magic you bring to the experience.

HAPPY Thoughts

HAPPY HINT #8: MOVE YOUR BODY

A HAPPY body plays a huge role in a HAPPY life. Your body—your *meat suit*—exists to embrace physical experiences. And movement, in some form, is essential for those experiences to take place.

My physical therapist once told me that *Motion is the lotion*, and I've never forgotten the image that popped into my mind. I pictured my body with a giant smiley face for a head, while someone beside me—holding an oversized lotion bottle labeled "motion"—helped me apply the magic that put that smile in place.

In essence, Movement brings your body Joy. It not only keeps everything functioning properly but also improves your mood and sleep. Movement—also known as exercise—enhances your overall well-being, both physically and emotionally.

The best part? Movement is highly personal, and ANY AMOUNT can bring happiness to your body. At my lowest physically, there were days when the only thing I could voluntarily move was my face—so I did. Simply opening and closing my eyes brought me great joy as I took in the beautiful colors of my room and watched Hallmark movies on TV. Since then, I've regained some strength and agility, and I revel in my ability to hula hoop—a movement activity I've loved since childhood.

Your mission, with this HAPPY Hint, is to move in a way that makes YOUR body HAPPY. Find a way to apply the *Motion Lotion*, creating smiles your body can feel—inside and out.

HAPPY Thoughts

HAPPY HINT #9: KEEP YOUR EYES ON THE HAPPY PRIZE

This HAPPY Hint is all about envisioning your HAPPY Place. Whether physical or virtual, having a HAPPY Place provides a personal haven whenever you need or want an escape. It's a private space for you to enjoy—your HAPPY little secret.

When creating a physical HAPPY Place, visual aesthetics play a key role. You want your space filled with colors, knick-knacks, and decorations that bring you a sense of calm and peace. At the same time, it's important to avoid anything that induces stress or anxiety.

Your physical HAPPY Place can be found in nature or within a man-made space. Perhaps a babbling brook in a nearby forest meets your HAPPY Place requirements. Or maybe you'd prefer to transform a section of your garage into your dedicated sanctuary of smiles.

A virtual HAPPY Place follows the same concept but exists without physical components. Entire virtual worlds on the internet may be worth exploring. Another option is to check out some virtual reality goggles.

However, imagination is the ultimate virtual HAPPY Place creator—it's always with you and accessible anywhere. Best of all, your imagination allows you to tap into limitless potential, creating as many different HAPPY Place*s* as you desire, each one as unique as you are!

My HAPPY Places have included both physical and virtual spaces. Currently, my physical HAPPY Place is my bedroom—also known as my *Creation Station*. Before moving into my new house, I intentionally chose curtains and bedding that would bring a smile to my face every time I walked into the room. On my bookcase, I've placed pictures of loved ones, gifts from dear friends and family, and mementos that remind me of my favorite holidays—all of which spark feelings of Love, Joy, and Appreciation whenever I see them.

During my worst periods of illness, I had no physical

HAPPY Place. I felt like a prisoner to excruciating pain and indescribable exhaustion. But I thank the Universe every day for the gift of my imagination. It allowed me to escape my physical prison and visit my virtual HAPPY Places anytime, anywhere.

The place I visited most often was a vast field with endless shades of green grass. It was filled with countless flowers—each a different shape, size, and color. The two types that stood out most were tulips and sunflowers. This virtual HAPPY Place became my saving grace, always summoning feelings of Peace, Joy, Abundance, and Appreciation.

So, how will you envision your HAPPY Place? Will it be physical, virtual, or both?

Whichever you choose, always *Keep Your Eyes On The HAPPY Prize!*

HAPPY Thoughts

HAPPY HINT #10: STOP AND SMELL THE HAPPY

The nose knows—am I right?

Some scents lure you in with their deliciousness, while others make you gag. Certain odors even serve as built-in warning systems, signaling situations to avoid. For this HAPPY Hint, your challenge is to satisfy your sniffer and celebrate the fragrances that bring a smile to your face.

What fascinates me is how the sense of smell can activate the HAPPY both in the present and the past. For example, the appetizing aromas in a café can spark wide-mouthed grins as fresh-baked desserts emerge from the oven. Yet, those same scents can also bring joy by conjuring up delightful memories of people, places, and moments from the past. In essence, embracing this HAPPY Hint can double the joy you experience.

One of my favorite ways to *Stop And Smell The HAPPY* is by lighting scented candles. I have a nice assortment that I rotate throughout the year based on the season, my mood, or the occasion. Not only do I love experiencing a variety of scents, but I also enjoy experimenting with new ones.

For example, my summertime favorites include fresh, fruity fragrances, while fall and winter call for deeper, woodsy, and earthy aromas. When I'm writing or creating, I prefer scents that stimulate my mind and sharpen my focus, like white tea and sage. And when it's time to unwind, a eucalyptus spearmint candle soothes my soul.

Even at my lowest points physically, I would ask someone to light a scented candle in my room. The aroma helped calm and comfort me, promoting feelings of positivity and well-being. Certain scents from those candles would stir up HAPPY memories, leaving me no choice but to smile.

So, how will you follow your nose?

Maybe you'll stop by the mall food court and breathe in the mouth-watering aromas of freshly prepared dishes.

Or perhaps you'll take a literal approach and stop to smell the roses—or any other fragrant flower.

The key to this HAPPY Hint is simple: let your nose lead the way!

HAPPY Thoughts

HAPPY HINT #11: HEAR AND/ OR FEEL THE HAPPY VIBES

Music possesses a unique ability to activate the HAPPY through sound, touch, and memory. Its joyful vibrations travel through our ears and skin, allowing us to both hear and feel its goodness. And just like HAPPY smells, HAPPY songs can evoke delightful memories of people, places, and experiences from the past. Through lyrics, melodies, and beats, music has the power to bring happiness into our lives in countless ways.

With this HAPPY Hint, your invitation is to listen to and/or feel the vibrations of songs that bring a smile to your face. Maybe you've created an upbeat, cheerful playlist that's perfect for your commute. Or perhaps you'll search HAPPY Vibes on your music app and explore the recommendations. What matters most is that these HAPPY vibes are flowing into your system in some way.

I practice this HAPPY Hint while exercising after my wake-up stretches. I found a Spotify playlist called HAPPY that features countless songs with uplifting, inspiring, and motivating beats. Listening to and feeling my HAPPY playlist helps me embrace the day with a joyful heart. And when I glance at the songs, a smile (and sometimes even a laugh) creeps onto my face as fond memories come to life.

Now it's your turn to experience the HAPPY vibes!

Listen, Feel, and Relive the joy contained in your favorite songs—I bet you'll be smiling in no time!

HAPPY Thoughts

HAPPY HINT #12: THROW A PARTY FOR YOUR PALATE

Yummy, yummy for the tummy!

Eating can be a delightful experience, especially when you're not rushed and can truly savor each bite. With so many flavors—sweet, salty, bitter, savory, and spicy—mixing and mingling, it's like throwing a party for your taste buds!

Your mission with this HAPPY Hint, should you choose to accept it, is to *Throw A Party For Your Palate.* Treat yourself and take pleasure in a delicious snack or meal. It can be as simple or extravagant as you wish. You can create it yourself or have someone prepare it for you. The key ingredient to this HAPPY Hint is fully engaging your sense of taste.

Food is my love language. My tummy lives by trying new flavors and smiles with every new experience. There are very few things I don't (or won't) eat and enjoy, so *Throw A Party For Your Palate* is one of the easiest HAPPY Hints for me to embrace.

What about you? What flavors make your taste buds HAPPY? What delicious snacks or meals will you include as you throw your palate a HAPPY party?

HAPPY Thoughts

HAPPY HINT #13: HONOR YOUR AWESOMENESS

Have you ever found yourself waiting for a special occasion to use something—only to realize you're still waiting?

With this HAPPY Hint, I urge you to STOP! Stop waiting, my dear friend. The special occasion is YOU, and the day is TODAY!

Celebration is the secret to this HAPPY Hint. And you are here to celebrate everything that makes you YOU. You are a magnificent, one-in-eight-billion kind of miracle—worthy of Love, Joy, and Self-Appreciation.

It's time to dress up in your favorite or fanciest outfit. Use the good stuff you've been saving for a special occasion. Pin a bright, bold flower in your hair or on your shirt collar. Even on a quiet night at home, style your hair as if you were heading to a party. The ways to *Honor Your Awesomeness* are limitless—it's all up to your imagination and how you choose to celebrate the beautiful BEing that is YOU!

For me, honoring my awesomeness often means accessorizing with bright colors. I love painting my toenails to match the seasons and holidays. I also adore the vibrant beauty of Mother Nature's flowers and seize every opportunity to pick one—to wear in my hair or tuck behind my ear. *But one of my all-time favorite ways to honor my awesomeness?* Wearing bright, sparkly shirts. Nothing says celebration to me quite like a little sparkle!

So, are you ready to STOP WAITING and START CELEBRATING?

The time is now to embrace what makes you feel special and *Honor Your Awesomeness*. Because YOU, my friend, are ABSOLUTELY AMAZING!

HAPPY Thoughts

HAPPY HINT #14: VENTURE OUTSIDE

Exposure to Mother Nature and the elements is directly linked to increased happiness. Sunlight activates serotonin, the *HAPPY Hormone*. The rhythmic pitter-patter of raindrops can bring a deep sense of peace, while a cool breeze can awaken your soul and make you feel alive. All this—and more—awaits when you *Venture Outside*.

There's something undeniably magical about shifting your surroundings from indoors to outdoors. The constant hum of busy-ness fades, replaced by a sense of freedom. You can Breathe, Create, Think, Not Think,

Feel, Play, and simply BE. Picture the pure, unbridled joy of children romping at recess, and you'll know exactly what I mean.

I take great pleasure in BEing outdoors whenever possible. At my lowest physically, that meant nothing more than having someone roll me and my wheelchair onto the patio for as long as I could tolerate. At my fittest, you'd find me running miles daily, training for cross-country meets. These days, I bask in the great outdoors by walking through my neighborhood or simply sitting on the back patio, soaking up the miraculous pond in my backyard and all its wildlife. No matter how I'm feeling, *Venturing Outside*—especially into the sunlight—elevates my happiness and brings my soul to life.

With this HAPPY Hint, I invite you to intentionally carve out time in nature. Take your lunch break on a bench outside. Jump in some puddles during or after a rainstorm. Or, like me, find a moment to sit and just BE.

The secret to this HAPPY Hint isn't how much time you spend outside—it's simply making the time. Once you start, you'll likely crave more. Let Mother Nature work her magic, and watch your happiness levels soar!

HAPPY Thoughts

HAPPY HINT #15: REST, RELAX, RENEW, RECEIVE

I'm sure you've heard the cliché You can't pour from an empty cup.

And if you haven't, it simply means you must prioritize self-care before you can fully support others. While this saying is spot on, I'll take it a step further—self-care is essential even if you're *not* in a caregiving role. It's *not* selfish; it's necessary for your happiness and well-being.

Rest, Relaxation, Renewal, and Receiving are all key aspects of self-care worth exploring. *Rest* means listening to your body and taking a physical break, honoring its need to recover. *Relaxation* is more of a mental reset, a chance for your mind to unwind from the constant busy-ness of life. *Renewal* combines both the physical and mental, a recharging of your body and soul. And *Receiving* simply means allowing—allowing yourself to experience the benefits of self-care and all the joy it brings.

I won't lie. This HAPPY Hint was a tough one for me in the past. As a former perfectionist, I felt the need to always be busy—moving, thinking, planning, creating. If I wasn't, both subconsciously and consciously, I felt lazy or guilty. I rarely gave my body and mind the time they needed to recharge and function properly.

But prioritizing self-care has changed my life in countless ways. My body and brain thank me daily for giving them the chance to *Rest, Relax,* and *Renew*. My body rewards me with greater strength, endurance, mobility, and energy. My mind honors me with inspiration and creativity. And by choosing to *Receive* and allow, these gifts come with far more ease and flow than when I was stuck in the cycle of endless busy-ness.

So, how will you invite more self-care into your world? Are you ready to Rest, Relax, Renew, and Receive?

HAPPY Thoughts

HAPPY HINT #16: CREATE A POSITIVITY WORD BANK

Words have power—they can shape your happiness, for better or worse. They have the ability to encourage, empower, and uplift, or to discourage, demoralize, and tear down. And whether you realize it or not YOUR OWN WORDS influence your joy more than anyone else's.

Why? Because you are the only person who is with you at all times. You speak words aloud, write or type them, and think them—both consciously and unconsciously—all day, every day. That's why it's so important for your well-being that your words be as Kind, Gentle, and

Compassionate as possible.

With this HAPPY Hint, I invite you to *Create a Positivity Word Bank*—a collection of feel-good words that evoke positivity through their meaning, feeling, or association. Think of it as an arsenal of goodness, ready to lift your spirits, remind you of joy, and help you infuse more loving words into your life.

How do you create a Positivity Word Bank?

By playing word games, of course! Below, I've outlined two fun ways to get your creative juices flowing. I used the word Happiness as an example, but feel free to choose any positive word you like. While these games are based on the English alphabet, you can play in any language you prefer.

LET THE GAMES BEGIN!

<u>Word Game #1: Meaning & Feeling</u>

    1. Choose a positive word you'd like to explore and write it down.

    2. Go through the alphabet and list a word—starting with each letter—that either *means* or *evokes the feeling* of your initial word.

Example: Initial word = Happiness
- A = **Appreciation**

- B = **Bliss**
- C = **Celebration**
- D = **Delight**
- E = **Enjoyment**

Word Game #2: Association

1. Choose a positive word you'd like to explore and write it down.

2. Go through the alphabet and list a word—starting with each letter—that you *associate* with your initial word.

Example: Initial word = Happiness
- A = **Animals**
- B = **Birthdays**
- C = **Connection**
- D = **Delicious**
- E = **Expansive**

*For an extra dose of HAPPY, play another round using a different positive word. And when you're done, add your *Positivity Word Bank* to your *HAPPY Box* for future smiles and inspiration!

HAPPY Thoughts

HAPPY HINT #17: GIVE YOURSELF A LOVE NOTE OR LETTER

Have you ever received a Valentine or a note sent from a secret admirer?

If so, chances are your heart felt all warm and fuzzy, and your face lit up with a smile. If not—well, now is your moment to experience that joy for yourself!

Because you're about to *Love On Yourself* in a big way— using the power of positive words!

Embracing This HAPPY Hint

Take a moment to celebrate you—all the things that make you special, inside and out. Think about both your BEing qualities (who you are and what you are about) and your DOing qualities (what you do and how you do it). This love letter is about the *whole you*—the incredible, one-of-a-kind package that YOU are.

If this feels tricky or you hit a case of writer's block, think about what your closest friends and family say they love about you. And if you feel a little silly—that's totally normal! Most of us weren't taught to appreciate ourselves this way. So, pretend you're writing to your best friend—because, in reality, YOU ARE!

Make It Easy With A Brainstorm

To make this HAPPY Hint even more fun, start with a simple brainstorming session. Create categories and list aspects you love about yourself under each one.

For example:
- **Outer beauty** – My smile
- **Inner beauty** – My kind heart
- **DOing quality** – Bringing happiness to others
- **BEing quality** – A loyal friend

The Love Note Or Love Letter

Once you've got your list, it's time to put it all together in a heartfelt note or letter. Write it as if you're speaking to someone you deeply care about—because that someone is YOU!

Here's an example:

Dear Amanda,

Your smile is so shiny and bright—it lights up a room the moment you walk in. Your big heart has space for everyone you meet, and I am so proud of the way you bring joy to others, no matter what's happening around you. You always *Find the HAPPY in the Crappy*, and that's such a rare and wonderful gift.

But what I admire most about you is your ability to be a truly great friend. You listen with your whole heart, support and encourage others, and create a safe space where people feel seen and heard—without judgment. You are the best cheerleader around!

I love you so much—every single bit of you.

Hugs and Smiles,
Yours Truly

What to Do with Your Love Note or Love Letter

Once you've written your note or letter, you might want to:

- **Seal it up and mail it to yourself.** Imagine the joy of receiving such a heartfelt, uplifting piece of mail!
- **Display it in your room.** A daily visual reminder of your self-love is a powerful mood booster.
- **Tuck it into your *HAPPY Box*.** What a beautiful addition to your collection of cheerful treasures!

No matter where you keep it, be sure to reread it often. This love letter holds a unique magic—bringing you a level of joy no one else can. After all, it's the most perfect, personal, profession of love there is!

HAPPY Thoughts

HAPPY HINT #18: LET YOUR INNER ARTIST SHINE

Who's ready to color outside of the lines?

It's time to let Imagination and Creativity take the wheel and bring more HAPPY into your world. Whether you realize it or not, you are an artist—and your life is your greatest masterpiece. Everything about you—how you look, think, speak, and act—adds to your ever-evolving canvas.

This HAPPY Hint encourages you to *Let Your Inner Artist Shine* by exploring new ways to invite more Creativity and Imagination into your life. Think about how HAPPY little kids are when they're handed a blank sheet of paper and a box of colors—free to create without limits. This is your chance to color outside the lines without fear of judgment...especially from yourself.

I personally love the magic of imagination and creation. Give me a pen and a notebook, and I can get lost for hours—writing stories, journaling, and doodling. Putting pen to paper allows me to express myself, create impact, and unwind. Writing, in all its forms, boosts my happiness levels.

Creating with color also brings me joy. My *Designated Fun Bag* is packed with all my favorite coloring supplies—gel pens, glitter pens, crayons, colored pencils, and markers in endless hues, shades, tints, and tones. My go-to coloring books feature uplifting words and phrases, surrounded by playful designs of all shapes and sizes. The mix of vibrant colors and heartwarming messages always brings a satisfied smile to this artist's face.

So, how will you Let Your Inner Artist Shine?

Writing, coloring, painting, sculpting, music, theater, film, dance, crafting—any creative outlet—engages your imagination and gets your creative juices flowing. And when you're in that artistic flow, you open yourself up to receiving even more HAPPY.

Go ahead—embrace your inner artist. The world is your canvas!

HAPPY Thoughts

HAPPY HINT #19: DREAM BIG

You may have heard a friend proclaim, *Never in my wildest dreams did I expect that to happen*! You may have even caught yourself saying these words, emphasizing how unlikely it seemed to achieve a certain goal.

My question to you is this:

WHY NOT?

You, dear friend, are the creator of your own happiness —and Big, Wild Dreams play a huge role in that. Dreams provide a delightful destination, both literally and figuratively. Maybe your dream is to live on a quiet island beach. Or perhaps you aspire to run your own business. Whatever it may be, dreams accompany you on your journey, offering Hope, Affirmation, and Something to Look Forward to.

But dreaming isn't just about reaching a goal—it's also about the joy of dreaming itself. It engages the imagination and expands the heart, mind, and spirit. Dreams make EVERYTHING possible!

When my biggest dream came true, I caught myself saying, *Never in my wildest dreams did I expect to walk independently again.*

For fifteen years, the idea of taking steps on my own lifted my spirits on my worst days. And on my best days, it fueled my determination to build strength, endurance, and mobility. My Big, Wild Dream of walking unassisted remained in my heart, mind, body, and spirit—until it became a reality.

And with that experience, I found myself asking the same question I posed to you earlier:

WHY NOT in my wildest dreams?

If my Biggest, Wildest Dream could come true, then I had to wonder:

What else is possible?

With this HAPPY Hint, I invite you to Imagine the Impossible and *Dream Big.* Think about what you want or desire most, and ask yourself:

What's the BEST thing that could happen?

Or simply dream for the sake of dreaming. Whether it's a means to an end or the end itself, *Dreaming Big* holds the key to creating your happiness.

HAPPY Thoughts

HAPPY HINT #20: SCHEDULE A HAPPINESS CHECK-IN

To track progress, businesses often conduct quarterly or annual reviews. These meetings highlight what's working, what's not, and help identify future goals and challenges. They're essential for the growth and vitality of any organization.

A *Happiness Check-In* follows a similar concept—but instead of focusing on numbers, facts, and figures, it centers on emotions and personal well-being.

Building on *HAPPY Hint #1: Get Curious About Your Own Happiness*, this HAPPY Hint encourages you to schedule regular moments of self-reflection. Your *Happiness Check-In* could happen quarterly or annually—just like a business review—or even daily, if that suits you best. What matters most is choosing a rhythm that gives you time to Pause, Reflect, and Intentionally Focus on your happiness.

Once you've set a schedule, mark it on your calendar. After completing today's *Happiness Check-In*, that future date becomes your next opportunity to reconnect with yourself and all things HAPPY.

Since this practice can cover a lot, here are some basic questions I use during my own *Happiness Check-In* to help you get started. You'll also find these in the *HAPPY Thoughts* section following this hint:

1. On a scale of 1 to 5-- How HAPPY do I feel right now?
(1 being the *least* HAPPY and 5 being the *most* HAPPY)

2. At this moment, what brings a smile to my face?

3. What activities or habits currently bring me joy?

4. In what areas of my life could I create more HAPPY?

—Business/Career/Education
—Finances
—Health/Wellbeing
—Family/Friends/Pets
—Romance
—Personal Growth

—Fun/Recreation
—Physical Environment

5. What changes could I make to elevate my happiness level?

Personally, I find Happiness Check-Ins especially helpful at the start or end of the year. They align perfectly with my year-end journaling and give me momentum to begin the new year on a HAPPY note. Plus, it's an easy timeframe to remember—especially for someone like me, who tends to forget dates and isn't exactly a big planner.

Now it's your turn.

Here's to the Happiness Check-In—may it give you the chance to Pause, Reflect, and Intentionally Focus on your HAPPY!

* For an extra boost of HAPPY, save all your Happiness Check-Ins. Each time you complete a new one, revisit your past entries and notice how you've grown from check-in to check-in.

HAPPY Thoughts

Happiness Check-In Questions:

(1) On a scale of 1 to 5—How HAPPY do I feel right now?
*** 1 being the least HAPPY and 5 being the most HAPPY ***

(2) At this moment, what brings a smile to my face?

(3) What activities or habits currently bring me joy?

(4) In what areas of my life could I create more HAPPY?

- Business/Career/Education.
- Finances
- Health/Wellbeing
- Family/Friends/Pets
- Romance
- Personal Growth
- Fun/Recreation
- Physical Environment

(5) What changes could I make to elevate my happiness level?

HAPPY Thoughts

HAPPY HINT #21: BE PRESENT

BEing present is a gift!

It's a Wholehearted, In-The-Moment, Mind-Body-Spirit Synchronistic experience. Many athletes describe it as BEing "in the zone". The gift of presence increases your ability to receive all the things that are meant for you—especially happiness.

So, how does BEing present actually work?

It involves Mindfulness, Awareness, and a Deep Connection to both yourself and your surroundings.

It means intentionally observing the current moment —without judgment. It's about actively noticing your thoughts, feelings, and environment, rather than getting swept away by distractions. When it comes to BEing Present, focus is your friend.

At my last job—before I became severely and chronically ill—I was a habitual multitasker. My desk was constantly covered with three or four projects I was juggling at once, all while answering phones. It looked like that during lunch breaks too…even during our monthly birthday parties. I was efficient, I got things done, and I genuinely *thought* I was HAPPY and having fun.

But everything shifted as my health declined and I lost the ability to multitask. Forced to slow down—both physically and mentally—I had no choice but to focus on one thing at a time. That's when I started to notice real change. I made fewer careless mistakes. I no longer had to double or triple-check my work. I felt more engaged with my clients. I actually *tasted* my lunch. And I ended up having *way* more fun at our birthday celebrations!

Monotasking brought me greater mindfulness, awareness, and connection to myself and the world around me. It helped me become more present. *BEing Present* put me back "in the zone" at work. *And honestly?* If it weren't for the rapid decline in my physical and mental health, I would've said those last few months at that job were the happiest.

So, how will you BE more Present?

Whatever path you choose, remember to embrace the power of Mindfulness, Awareness, and Meaningful Connection —to yourself and your surroundings.

HAPPY Thoughts

HAPPY HINT #22: LITERALLY LAUGH OUT LOUD

It's no coincidence that the emoji most used for "LOL" (laugh out loud) is the smiling face with tears of joy.

Laughter is cathartic. It often leaves us feeling Lighter, Brighter, and more Positive. It also delivers a whole bunch of physical benefits—like lowering blood pressure, tightening the abs, and triggering the release of the brain's feel-good chemicals, which help relieve pain and fight illness. One study even found that just 10 to 15 minutes of laughter a day can burn up to 40 calories. Whether you're looking to boost your mind, body, or spirit, laughter truly has medicinal properties —just like the famous quote suggests.

Laughter has always played a big role in my life and has always been able to boost my mood. On countless occasions, I'd burst into spontaneous fits of laughter that my parents and I lovingly called *laugh attacks*. One especially memorable moment happened at a high school retreat, where I had a *laugh attack* that lasted for hours. My friends thought it was hilarious and kept fueling it with jokes, silly faces, and ridiculous dances—adding to my little bubble of joy (and probably helping me burn a ton of calories).

Even during my lowest physical points, laughter gave me a much-needed escape from chronic joint and muscle pain. My care workers would often share funny stories from their lives to make me giggle. We'd search for comedies or animated films—especially the ones with talking animals (my absolute favorites!). And even if the joy lasted only a few seconds, that little burst of laughter could completely shift my mood—in mind, body, and spirit.

Now it's your turn to lean into the laughter!

With this HAPPY Hint, I invite you to *Literally Laugh Out Loud.* Belt out a big ol' belly laugh and let those tears of joy flow freely. Watch a stand-up comedy special on YouTube. Grab a joke book from your local library. Or better yet, *Literally Laugh Out Loud* the next time you do something delightfully silly.

When it comes to this HAPPY Hint, remember:

Bringing laughs brings Joy—to your mind, body, and spirit.

HAPPY Thoughts

HAPPY HINT #23: PLAY

"People tend to forget that play is serious"
—David Hockney

Play is an essential piece of the happiness puzzle. Its magic transcends definition and is best embraced through experience, whether observed or lived. Just watch children at recess, in parks, or on playgrounds —shrieking with delight as they engage in activities purely for enjoyment. That, right there, is the power of *Play*.

Too often, in our busy, hustle-filled lives, *Play* becomes an afterthought—or worse, it's discouraged altogether.

But *Play* absolutely has its place, especially when it comes to boosting happiness. Engaging in activities purely for the joy of them can lift your mood and, depending on the activity, provide physical health benefits too. *Play* also sparks the imagination—a fertile space for creativity and inspiration. It's not just fun; it's practical. For the well-being of your mind, body, and spirit, normalizing *Play* in daily life might just be one of the happiest choices you can make.

If you find this HAPPY Hint a bit challenging, I totally get it. As a former perfectionist, I wasn't exactly wired to prioritize playtime as a daily experience. I treated *Play* like a reward—something reserved for weekends after working hard all week. And when I did allow myself a bit of fun during the week, I *Had-To* make sure all my work was done first.

These days, I see *Play* and work through a completely different lens. I've redefined them to fit inside my own *HAPPY Bubble*. To me, both represent meaningful activities that I was put here to do—and both deserve a place in my daily life.

I embrace this HAPPY Hint through both observation and participation. As I mentioned earlier, I absolutely adore watching children at *Play*—their contagious energy lifts my spirits, no matter what mood I'm in. *And when it comes to participating?* Coloring, hula hooping, dancing around my kitchen, and trying to entice my cat (Pinky Beans) to *Play* with his toys are just a few of my favorite ways to dive into playtime.

So, how will you bring this HAPPY Hint to life? Are there activities you once loved that you haven't done in a while? I'd suggest playing around with those ideas first.

However you choose to *Play*, remember this:

Play is both Fun and Functional—good for the mind, body, spirit, and your overall happiness.

HAPPY Thoughts

HAPPY HINT #24: TRY SOMETHING NEW

Infinite amounts of pleasurable experiences are out there—just waiting to bring you smiles.

So how do you discover what they have to offer? Simple: you *Get-To* feed your curiosity and *Try Something New*.

I like to think of this HAPPY Hint like test-driving cars at a dealership or sampling goodies at your local market. It's a fabulous way to get a taste of something different. If it brings you joy—fantastic! If it's not for you—that's totally okay. Just move on and try something else.

No matter what the salesperson or vendor might think, you're under no obligation to buy the car or the product—or in this case, to keep doing the new thing. This is a HAPPY opportunity to Broaden Your Horizons, Explore, and Discover.

For me, the entire process of creating this magical book embodies this very HAPPY Hint. I've always loved writing and have contributed chapters to several international best-selling multi-author books. *But creating a solo book?* That's been a longtime dream. So, at the end of last year, I decided to go for it—to *Try Something New*.

This delightful journey has been quite different from any of my previous writing experiences. I've approached this project with more intention and ceremony than ever before. Weekly calls with my publisher and fellow solo authors have provided encouragement, support, and a steady stream of inspiration. For the first time, I've also incorporated AI (artificial intelligence) as one of my many editing tools—an exciting addition to my creative process. And to top it all off, I've learned to use a book formatting program called *Kindle Create* to assemble these lovely pages and bring them to life.

Trying Something New has absolutely expanded my horizons—helping me Grow, Stretch, Explore, and Discover...all while bringing smiles along the way.

Now it's your turn!

Get out there and *Try Something New*. Test-drive the many experiences waiting to brighten your day. Who knows—you might just stumble upon your new favorite HAPPY Hobby!

HAPPY Thoughts

HAPPY HINT #25: PAUSE, BREATHE, APPRECIATE

Life is the happiest thing there is. But with all the ups, downs, twists, turns, and curveballs life tends to throw our way, we sometimes forget what a Magical, Exciting, Beautiful Adventure it truly is. Even when we factor in worst-case scenarios, there's still nothing more Miraculous than life itself!

With this HAPPY Hint, I invite you to REMEMBER—remember just how Glorious life is, no matter your current mood or situation. *Pause. Breathe. Appreciate.* And your happiness levels are sure to rise, even if only the tiniest bit.

Pausing, a key part of this HAPPY Hint, creates space—space to be present. Whether you're feeling low or vibing high, *Pausing* anchors you in the moment, free from attachments or expectations. So begin with a simple pause.

Breathing is the next essential step. Breath is life—YOUR life—and without it, you wouldn't BE. Take a deep breath. Feel it move through your body. Let it ground you in your aliveness.

Appreciating brings this HAPPY Hint full circle. Cherish the pause. Treasure your breath. Acknowledge this incredible truth: YOU…ARE…ALIVE.

Pause. Breathe. Appreciate. Together, these three small acts become a powerful reminder that life—in all its Messy, Wild, Wonderful Glory—is truly the happiest thing there is.

Embracing this HAPPY Hint offers comfort and clarity, especially in times of stress and overwhelming chaos. It was perfect during that moment in 2021, when my loved ones and I miraculously escaped a devastating house fire. A simple pause, as I looked around at the destruction that lay before me. A full-bodied breath of relief and release as I processed the fact that my loved ones and I were *still* alive. A sense of overwhelming Gratitude and Appreciation as I looked down at the pants I just happened to be wearing…a pair of black sweatpants with these three simple words:

LIFE…IS…GOOD.

I weave this HAPPY Hint into my days in many ways. I've built it into both my wake-up and bedtime routines, alongside my stretches and journaling. I even created a kind of random phone timer system, setting alarms at various times throughout the day. When they go off, I stop whatever I'm doing and simply: *Pause…Breathe…Appreciate.*

However and whenever you choose to embrace this HAPPY Hint, keep this in mind:

Pause, Breathe, and *Appreciate*…to REMEMBER how HAPPY life truly is.

HAPPY Thoughts

HAPPY HINT #26: CHOOSE JOY FOR YOURSELF

This is the last HAPPY Hint—focused on yourself—that I invite you to incorporate into your life. However, it's just the beginning of your never-ending journey in creating HAPPY Hints.

Make a conscious effort to choose happiness every day —REGARDLESS of your circumstances. This doesn't mean ignoring, suppressing, or denying negative situations and emotions; we are human, and these are part of life. What I'm suggesting is that you focus on the good and *Find the HAPPY in the Crappy* when life isn't ideal.

Embracing this HAPPY Hint may seem impractical, and you might feel uncertain or inept. The simplest way to overcome this resistance is to take it one step at a time. Start with the desire—*the simple desire*—to *want* to be HAPPY each day…no matter what.

Daily practice of this HAPPY Hint is highly recommended, even if it feels unnecessary. Without regular reinforcement, you may be surprised at how quickly it slips your mind. Along with repetition, accessibility is key. Consider leaving a sticky note in a spot you frequent as a reminder, or create a recording to play before bedtime.

Here's my practice to remind me to choose happiness every day: As part of my wake-up routine, while resting after my stretches and exercises, I affirm out loud to myself and the Universe, *Today I choose to be HAPPY*. Before bed, I repeat the mantra, replacing *today* with *tomorrow*.

When and how you apply this HAPPY Hint is up to you—just claim it loud and proud. And remember, repetition is key. Over time, you'll discover that you've created one of the most beautiful HAPPY habits there is.

HAPPY Thoughts

PART 2: SHARING YOUR HAPPY

*26 HAPPY Hints To Bring
More Joy To Others*

*Note: If For Some Reason You Are Unable To Enjoy These Happy Hints On Your Own, Ask Someone For Support—The More The Merrier!!

HAPPY HINT #1: GET CURIOUS ABOUT THE HAPPINESS OF THOSE AROUND YOU

The magical adventure of sharing your HAPPY with others begins when you become curious. Curiosity fosters Connection through Acknowledgment, Awareness, and Empathy. The more connected you are to others, the easier it is to bring them joy.

During the COVID-19 pandemic, I became deeply curious about the struggles of billions. It quickly became clear that what people longed for most was physical connection through hugs and smiles. Yet, with face masks covering our expressions and social distancing keeping us apart, those simple joys were out of reach. While I couldn't offer physical hugs or smiles, this realization inspired me to create a symbolic alternative—*S.H.A.P.E. Cards*. These small, business-like cards carried a HAPPY, Heartfelt, Handwritten message and could be passed out anywhere, anytime, to anybody.

With this HAPPY Hint, I encourage you to notice what brings happiness to the people around you. Observe, reflect, and process what you discover. There's no right or wrong way—this is your personal happiness journey.

So go ahead—get curious! The more you learn about others, the more happiness can grow.

HAPPY Thoughts

HAPPY HINT #2: GIVE A GRACIOUS GREETING

We all want to be seen, right?

And no, I'm not talking about social media visibility or celebrity status. I mean simply BEing acknowledged—as a living, breathing human BEing.

With this HAPPY Hint, I invite you to do just that: recognize a stranger for no other reason than their existence as a beautiful human. The next time you run errands, share a small greeting with someone you encounter. It could be a smile, a wave, or—my personal favorite—the universal head nod, the classic "what's up?".

I love greeting strangers. I try to smile at as many people as possible throughout the day. Waving at cars and neighbors while walking through my neighborhood is especially enjoyable. As I mentioned before, the universal head nod is my favorite—it's simple, effortless, and just plain fun. But what truly makes these greetings worthwhile are the smiles, waves, and nods I receive in return. In those moments, I know I'm sharing my HAPPY, and others are feeling genuinely seen.

Of course, sometimes you won't get a response, and that's okay. A *Gracious Greeting* can still have an impact in ways you may never realize.

For instance, a single smile once saved a man from suicide. That day, he had received two devastating phone calls—one from an angry, tyrannical boss and another from a friend who had just been diagnosed with AIDS. Overwhelmed by despair, he began contemplating how to end his life.

Then, as he walked through a crowded street, a woman intentionally caught his gaze and smiled. She didn't say a word—just greeted him with a smile. And that was enough. That small moment of acknowledgment gave him the strength to keep going.

However you choose to express this HAPPY Hint, know

that your *Gracious Greeting* can bring joy far beyond what you can imagine.

HAPPY Thoughts

HAPPY HINT #3: NURTURE WITH NATURE

How does one begin to describe Mother Nature and her limitless possibilities for shared happiness?

Nature, at its simplest, is the physical world and all its phenomena—everything that exists outside of human creation. With this definition, you can see that She both is and produces countless wonders that bring joy to billions. Her bounty offers endless opportunities to *Spread the HAPPY*—to others and with others.

Yet, a more complex and paradoxical truth about Nature, her extraordinary gifts, and your opportunities to share them also exists. While her abundance is seemingly limitless, the quality of each experience is uniquely finite. Nature has the power to create an infinite number of breathtaking moments, yet no two will ever BE exactly the same.

Take a sunrise, for example. There have been countless sunrises before, and there will BE countless more to come. But no sunrise will ever BE exactly like the one you see today. Even within a single sunrise, every shifting color, every fleeting shape in the clouds, every glimmer of light is an unrepeatable masterpiece. What a Marvelous, Magical, Mysterious, and Miraculous event—one that inspires Awe, Joy, and Delight. And how much greater that joy is when it is shared!

Nature brings me immense pleasure as I revel in Her beauty, magic, and mystery. Sunrises are breathtaking, but for me, sunsets hold even more significance—simply because I'm usually awake to enjoy them. Appreciating them with loved ones has become a cherished ritual. On evening walks, my parents and I often pause to admire the sky, pointing out the vibrant pinks, blues, purples, oranges, and yellows. We smile at the shifting clouds, imagining the animals they resemble before they dissolve into new forms. In these moments, we are not just observing Nature—we are *nurtured* by Her and with Her.

We are Present. We are Connected. We are HAPPY.

So, how do you plan to embrace Nature's gifts? And with

whom will you share them?
Perhaps you'll bring freshly picked flowers to brighten your office or stargaze with a loved one under the night sky.

However you choose to nurture and be nurtured by Nature, remember this:

Each Marvelous, Magical, Mysterious, and Miraculous moment happens only once. Take full advantage of it. Appreciate it. Share it.

HAPPY Thoughts

HAPPY HINT #4: SEND SOME SNAIL MAIL

Are you sick and tired of receiving nothing but bills and junk mail in your mailbox or at your local post office?

Chances are your friends, family, and loved ones feel the same way. *So why not brighten someone's day with the gift of some HAPPY mail?*

For the longest time, the Postal Service was the primary way people communicated across long distances. Handwritten letters traveled far and wide, carrying news and heartfelt messages. Though the process was slow—moving at a snail's pace—it was how people stayed connected with those they couldn't see often.

Today, with so many fast and convenient ways to keep in touch, letter writing has become rare. The Postal Service is now used mainly for bills and advertisements rather than personal correspondence. But with this Happy Hint, you're invited to change that by bringing back the joy of *Snail Mail*!

Personally, my favorite kind of *Snail Mail* to send is handwritten birthday cards. I love selecting a blank card with bright, bold colors and designs, and then sitting in quiet reflection as I craft a personal message just for the recipient. Adding multi-colored glitter pen accents and fun stickers makes it even more special. Before sealing the envelope, I often include a little extra Birthday Love—perhaps some confetti or tiny sparkles. As I drop the card in the mail, I imagine the recipient's surprise and excitement upon receiving it.

How will you embrace this Happy Hint and revive the lost art of letter writing?

Maybe you'll send well wishes to a child away at college, reconnect with an old friend, or, like me, spread Birthday Love through *Snail Mail*.

Whatever you choose, your happiness and smiles will literally travel for miles—one letter at a time!

HAPPY Thoughts

118

HAPPY HINT #5: START A MEANINGFUL CONVERSATION

For many of us, daily conversations are either short, sweet, and to the point or long and drawn out with little substance. Small talk like this is usually low-risk emotionally and doesn't often lead to deep connections.

I consider myself the queen of small talk. I'm the person in the elevator who says hello and comments on the weather, last night's game, or your lovely shirt. Particularly in these moments, I strive to make each encounter as Joyful and Meaningful as possible because I never know if I'll see these individuals again. And in its own way, small talk achieves that goal beautifully.

However, I also cherish meaningful conversations—especially with people I interact with regularly. These deeper discussions create opportunities for mutual understanding and personal growth, both individually and collectively.

I relish the connections that deep discussions foster. I delight in the wide range of emotions people share when they open their hearts. There's something so powerful and beautiful about the bonds that form through meaningful conversation.

With this Happy Hint, I encourage you to choose someone you like and interact with frequently. Make a conscious effort to move beyond small talk and initiate a deeper conversation. To keep it natural, start with a casual topic so you don't catch the person off guard. Then, look for opportunities to expand on it, guiding the discussion toward something more personal and reflective.

For example, it recently snowed in my state—a rare occurrence. After the snow melted, I could've simply made small talk with my neighbor about the unexpected weather and shared my excitement. But to take the conversation a little deeper, I followed up by asking if they had any HAPPY memories of snow days from their past.

The *Happy Hint* within this Happy Hint is simple: Start with lighthearted small talk, then expand on it in a way that adds depth and meaning.

And who knows? Starting A Meaningful Conversation may lead to finding your next Bestie.

HAPPY Thoughts

HAPPY HINT #6: CONGRATULATE SOMEONE ON A JOB WELL DONE

Celebration plays a vital role in our happiness. It's the final step in achieving a goal or fulfilling a desire. Taking the time to Appreciate and Celebrate what we've accomplished—not just the outcome, but also the steps it took to get there—creates Excitement and Joy. And that joy often fuels our *HAPPY Fire* to pursue future goals and desires.

Yet, we often overlook the importance of celebration. Too often, we achieve something and quickly move on to the next goal without taking a moment to acknowledge our success. We forget to give ourselves and others the recognition we deserve.

With this HAPPY Hint, I invite you to embrace the art of celebration. Spread your HAPPY and positive energy by recognizing someone's success. Maybe your partner just got a raise, and you want to cook them a special meal. Or perhaps your child passed an exam after weeks of studying, and you want to proudly display their achievement on the refrigerator.

The key to this Happy Hint is to congratulate with both words and actions. This *Celebration Combination* reinforces the message and often creates an even greater sense of Excitement, Accomplishment, and Fulfillment for the recipient. Keep in mind that celebrating doesn't have to cost anything—a high-five, a pat on the back, or even a simple smile can make all the difference!

I love celebrating my friends and family for their accomplishments. Sadly, my loved ones live all across the world and I can't typically celebrate with them in person. However, thanks to today's technology, I can send voice recordings, texts, and video messages of congratulations. We can even meet up in real-time via video chat. Using these tools allows me to celebrate meaningfully, even from a distance, by combining words and actions.

Celebration is essential to our happiness. We must

remember to enjoy the fruits of our labor. And by congratulating others—especially when we pair our words with thoughtful actions—we create even more joy, for both them and ourselves.

So, who are you going to Congratualte and Celebrate?

HAPPY Thoughts

HAPPY HINT #7: PARTICIPATE IN LOCAL HAPPY

Generally speaking, people who are active in their local communities tend to lead happier lives. This is largely because community involvement fosters a strong sense of connection. Connection is a key component of happiness, helping to combat feelings of loneliness and isolation. It also nurtures Trust, Unity, Compassion, Dependability, Pride, and Solidarity—just to name a few. These feelings often arise when people share similar lived experiences.

This HAPPY Hint encourages you to form or strengthen your bond with your local community—the place you call home. It's all about giving back, whether through your time, money, or material resources. You might choose to spread your HAPPY in a structured way, like volunteering at a soup kitchen. Or, you may prefer a more casual approach, such as buying a refreshing drink from the neighborhood kids at their makeshift lemonade stand. There's no *wrong* way to give.

Recently, I embraced the idea of *Participating in Local HAPPY* by combining two things I love: walking around my neighborhood and baking homemade chocolate chip cookies. For several days, I happily baked in my kitchen, then assembled cookie bags with bright, colorful notes wishing my neighbors a wonderful day. On delivery day, I walked up and down the street, attaching the cookie bags to mailboxes and enjoying cheerful conversations with my neighbors.

Now it's your turn!

How will you give back to your local community and Spread the HAPPY?

HAPPY Thoughts

HAPPY HINT #8: PARTICIPATE IN GLOBAL HAPPY

Just as giving back locally fosters happiness through connection, giving back globally does the same—on an even larger scale. *Participating in Global HAPPY* nurtures Trust, Unity, Compassion, Dependability, Pride, and Solidarity. But the impact of your shared HAPPY isn't confined to your street, neighborhood, city, state, or even country—it reaches people all over the world.

With this HAPPY Hint, I invite you to create or

strengthen your global ties. Contribute to a cause that lights you up inside, for giving back joyfully is the goal. You might take a structured approach, such as donating to an international organization. Or, if you prefer something more personal, you could become an international pen pal, exchanging letters with someone from another country. Whether you donate your time, money, or material resources, there's no single *right* way to give.

I've *Participated in Global HAPPY* both formally and casually. Supporting nonprofit organizations run by friends abroad has allowed me to share my HAPPY with orphaned children, pregnant teens, single mothers, widows, and the elderly in various ways. Beyond sending monetary donations when I can, I've also had the privilege of providing school supplies and clothing. On a more personal level, I created an international Facebook group dedicated to *Spreading the HAPPY*, where I've built meaningful global connections—turning strangers into close friends and friends into family.

Now it's your turn!

How will you embrace this HAPPY Hint and share your joy with the world?

HAPPY Thoughts

HAPPY HINT #9: OPEN A DOOR FOR SOMEONE

This is one of my favorite HAPPY Hints because it works both literally and metaphorically—allowing you to spread twice as much HAPPY!

Literally speaking, *Opening A Door For Someone* is a small yet meaningful act of kindness, demonstrating courtesy and respect. Holding a door wide open—regardless of who the person is or what stage of life they're in—shows acknowledgment and recognition. More often than not, this simple gesture brings a smile to someone's face.

Metaphorically speaking, *Opening A Door For Someone* means creating an opportunity. Embracing this HAPPY Hint in this way could mean mentoring a co-worker or classmate, referring a friend's new lawn care service to your neighbors, or helping someone take the next step toward their dreams. Opening doors for others Boosts their Confidence, Expresses Belief in their Abilities, and Encourages them to Embrace New Possibilities—all of which contribute to greater happiness.

I consider it an honor to open doors for people, both literally and metaphorically!

In the literal sense, physically opening doors—even for myself—has been a challenge over the years. Many doors to restaurants, stores, and even bathrooms are heavy, and I've often needed and received help. This has made me acutely aware of how much this small act of kindness matters. So when I come across a door that I *can* hold open for someone else, I jump at the chance.

Metaphorically, I love opening doors through referrals and recommendations. If I discover a great new restaurant, you'll hear all about it. If you want to write a book, I can connect you with publishers. *Looking for ways to give back?* I know amazing nonprofit organizations that could use your help. Opening doors is all about connecting people in my circle with opportunities that align with their talents and gifts.

So, will you be on the lookout for literal doors to open throughout your day? Or will you take the metaphorical route and introduce someone to an opportunity that could change their life?

Either way, by recognizing and acknowledging others, you'll undoubtedly *Spread the HAPPY!*

HAPPY Thoughts

HAPPY HINT #10: PAY A GENUINE COMPLIMENT

Compliments—words of praise and admiration—can elevate someone's happiness in countless ways. They Boost Confidence, Enhance Self-esteem, and Provide Affirmation and Validation.

But only if they are genuine!

People can tell the difference between real and fake compliments. Yet, for various reasons, some resort to flattery that isn't entirely sincere. Maybe they want or need something from a particular person. Perhaps they're trying to spare someone's feelings or simply saying what they think the other person wants to hear.

On the flip side, many people hold back their compliments altogether. They might feel too shy or awkward to approach a stranger. The setting may seem inappropriate, or they may second-guess whether their words are welcome. There are countless reasons why people hesitate, even when they genuinely admire something about someone.

I have never been one to keep my compliments inside. I've been known to embarrass my friends and family by walking up to complete strangers just to tell them how much I love their hair color, their outfit, or their smile. If I admire something about someone, I make sure they know—right then and there.

That said, as a former people-pleaser, I did struggle with giving slightly exaggerated compliments. It wasn't that my admiration was false, but I had a habit of embellishing just a bit to make others feel good. Those days are behind me. Now, if you get a compliment from me, you better believe it's one hundred percent Genuine and Sincere.

And just like me, this HAPPY Hint encourages you to be completely real with your compliments. Resist the urge to flatter just to gain favor, and don't embellish your words to please others. Be bold. Praise and admire whoever, whenever, and wherever—but always make sure it comes straight from the heart.

Because when a compliment is real, there's never a wrong time or place to give it!

HAPPY Thoughts

HAPPY HINT #11: TAKE OR BE PART OF A GROUP PHOTO

Say cheese!

It's time to flash those pearly whites and make funny faces with friends for the camera. Or, if you prefer a more low-key approach to this HAPPY Hint, simply snap a quick picture with your Bestie the next time you hang out.

Taking group photos to commemorate fun times is a fantastic way to *Spread the HAPPY* with others. It's the perfect opportunity to capture and share the joy of the moment. Plus, those smiles don't just stay in the present; they can bring happiness in the future and even stir up memories from the past.

Group photos come in all shapes and sizes. Some are large and somewhat staged, like at weddings or family reunions. Others happen in the blink of an eye—like pulling out your phone for a quick shot with your partner at dinner. Whether planned or spontaneous, and no matter the size of the group, there's something special about the connection created in that moment. And when the photo is shared, the happiness spreads even further.

I love group photos—or *groupies*, as I jokingly call them. As a highly visual person, seeing myself in a group shot almost always transports me back to that exact moment. And when the people in the picture are dear to my heart, the joy is even greater.

Recently, I took part in a pretty large group photo at my elementary school reunion. Teachers and classmates I hadn't seen in nearly thirty years gathered together to say cheese for the cameras. Smiles, hugs, and stories were exchanged as we all posed—capturing not just the moment, but a lifetime of memories.

That photo doesn't just remind me of the fun I had at the reunion; it also brings back cherished memories of our school days. *And what's even better?* After a friend posted the picture on social media, nearly everyone in it shared the same reaction—HAPPY for both the present moment and the past.

That said, I have a soft spot for spontaneous *groupies*, especially with just one or two people. I love capturing random moments of joy—or being captured in them! Recently, a dear friend visited, and we spent a beautiful day walking through a nature preserve and along the lakefront. Out of nowhere, she pulled out her phone and snapped a few shots of us among the trees and beneath a stunning sunset. These photos will bring us joy now—and for years to come.

Now it's your turn!

How will you strike a pose? Will you go for a big group photo or keep it small and intimate?

Whatever you decide, have fun with this HAPPY Hint. And don't forget to share your group picture—because that's how smiles get spread for miles!

HAPPY Thoughts

HAPPY HINT #12: PHONE A FRIEND OR LOVED ONE

I just called to say I love you.
I just called to say how much I care.
I just called to say I love you.
And I mean it from the bottom of my heart.

These lyrics from Stevie Wonder play soulfully in my head, heart, and spirit whenever I think of this HAPPY Hint. It's an invitation to use your voice to *Spread the HAPPY* to a friend or loved one. Pick up the phone and share the love—simply call to tell someone you love or care about them. Imagine their surprise and joy when they hear those magical words, spoken straight from your heart.

I'll admit, this HAPPY Hint is a bit of a challenge for me. I'm not someone who readily talks on the phone. Due to memory, concentration, and focus issues, I communicate better when I can see the person or follow a back-and-forth conversation through text or messaging. So, when I do reach out by phone—especially to express my love—I'm stepping way out of my comfort zone. More often than not, the person on the other end of the call knows this, which only amplifies the HAPPY being shared.

Whether you're someone who talks on the phone all the time or, like me, use it sparingly, reaching out to a friend or loved one this way is a special, HAPPY treat. Much like the art of *Snail Mail*, meaningful conversation is a rare and welcome break from spam calls and robotic sales pitches. And when those words —*I love you* or *I care about you*—come from someone near and dear, it's the icing on the happiness cake!

*For an extra sprinkle of HAPPY, consider telling your friend or loved one *why* you love or care about them. That's the cherry on top of this happiness-filled moment!

HAPPY Thoughts

HAPPY HINT #13: RECALL, REMEMBER, REMINISCE

Memories are powerful, and the feelings they carry are just as impactful. Sometimes, when we recall a past event, the emotions that arise can be just as intense as when the event actually occurred. How fortunate this is—especially when it comes to *Spreading the HAPPY* with others!

Imagine sharing a magnificent moment with someone, whether it was several months or even years ago. As you recall the details, your heart warms, your body feels light, and a big smile spreads across your face. With those memories and feelings in mind, you reach out to that person and remind *them* of that HAPPY time. *Recalling, Remembering,* and *Reminiscing* about the event with them is sure to spark the same joyful emotions once felt.

Facebook's Memories feature has allowed me to embrace this HAPPY Hint regularly. As posts and pictures resurface, the visuals instantly transport me back in time. One memory, in particular, recently brought on the *Happy Tears.*

A photo from March 2024 appeared—a snapshot from a life-changing retreat I attended in Sedona, Arizona. That retreat gifted me a miracle healing, allowing me to walk unassisted once again. To celebrate, two of my dearest friends and I took a selfie in the mountains, capturing a moment of pure joy.

Seeing that picture filled my heart with Love, Appreciation, and Pure Happiness. I reposted it—tagging all my retreat friends—and sent personal messages to those in the photo, reminiscing about that magical moment.

By the end of the day, the comments and replies were pouring in—so much Love, Excitement, and Joy. It was clear that everyone was celebrating the miracle all over again, just as we had last year.

I revel in the idea of *Recalling, Remembering,* and *Reminiscing,* to *Spread the HAPPY* with others. It creates a ripple effect of joy because once you start, it's hard to stop. After all, if you've found one merry moment to revisit, more are sure to follow—along with laughter, smiles, and other HAPPY activations.

So, are you ready to Recall, Remember, and Reminisce?

HAPPY Thoughts

HAPPY HINT #14: CREATE A NEW SHARED TRADITION

Honoring fun traditions can amplify the happiness shared between you and others, much like recalling a HAPPY memory. By repeating a ritual, you not only experience joy in the present but also revisit cherished moments from the past. Depending on how long the tradition has been around, there may even be people still present who first started it—which truly elevates the happiness factor.

With that in mind, could YOU be one of those people? An Innovator, a Creator, the next Happiness Trendsetter?

This HAPPY Hint invites you to create and share a new, fun tradition. It can be as simple as starting a weekly family game night or as elaborate as organizing a monthly potluck dinner for your entire community.

Over the past few years, my boyfriend and I have created a traveling tradition—taking road trips to a beautiful set of cabins in the woods of Hot Springs, Arkansas (United States). We fell in love with the cabins the first time we stumbled upon them, and we quickly became smitten with the charming little town.

Grilling dinners outdoors, building cozy fires, strolling through the property's forests, and soaking in the outdoor hot tubs have given us countless opportunities for fun, joy, and laughter. We've even made friends with the owners of a local deli and make a point to dine there every time we visit. Hot Springs has become our go-to destination for celebrating birthdays, special occasions, and holidays. This new tradition has created a multitude of magical memories that we will cherish forever.

Now, my *Happiness Trendsetters,* it's your turn to create a fun tradition to share with others!

Whether it involves a large group or just a few close friends, remember this:

You'll be *Spreading the HAPPY* far into the future as your shared tradition creates lasting moments of joy for everyone involved.

HAPPY Thoughts

HAPPY HINT #15: ACTIVELY LISTEN

Have you ever found yourself in the middle of a conversation, contemplating your next response, only to realize you missed half of what the other person was saying?

I've been there. And let me tell you—it wasn't exactly a HAPPY situation. I felt embarrassed and frustrated with myself for not paying attention. I scrambled to come up with a response, feeling overwhelmed and anxious. And to be honest, my reply probably added little value to the conversation.

Conversation plays a huge role in relationships—it's how ideas are shared, decisions are made, and feelings are expressed. Ideally, speaking and listening would be equally balanced. But more often than not, the talking side dominates. Many people focus on what they're saying while they're speaking—and what they're going to say next while someone else is talking.

With this HAPPY Hint, I encourage you to tip the scales in favor of listening. Be mindful and *Actively Listen* when someone else is speaking. Listen to understand them and their point of view—not just to respond.

Active listening fosters happier, healthier relationships. It ensures the speaker feels truly Acknowledged, Seen, and Heard. As the listener, you'll absorb the full message, allowing you to respond more thoughtfully. Regardless of the topic—or whether you agree—active listening deepens connections, which can lead to more joy.

So, let's *Actively Listen* and *Spread the HAPPY* by intentionally Acknowledging, Seeing, and Hearing those we engage with in conversation.

HAPPY Thoughts

HAPPY HINT #16: MIX AND MINGLE

Island Mentality, as a psychological concept, refers to people who isolate themselves and live as loners —"islands"—because they struggle to relate to others. But let's be honest: no one is truly an island. Humans are wired for connection. Even in our most solitary moments, we crave companionship. This need is essential for survival, well-being, and happiness. We're meant to do life together.

In *my* version of *Island Mentality*, though, it's quite the opposite. Picture a Hawaiian luau—a big, joyful gathering filled with feasting, music, and vibrant cultural performances. That's the vibe I'm talking about.

So, in the spirit of togetherness and my twist on *Island Mentality*, this HAPPY Hint invites you to *Mix And Mingle*. Put yourself out there—physically, virtually, or both. Say hello to a neighbor. Strike up a conversation with someone new. Join an online group that shares your interests—or shake things up and explore communities that are totally outside your usual circle. The more people you *Mix And Mingle* with, the more opportunities you create to *Spread the HAPPY*.

I love to *Mix And Mingle*, especially in person. At social events, you'll usually find me making the rounds, chatting with all kinds of people. I regularly put myself out there—smiling as I introduce myself to strangers.

And yes, *Mixing And Mingling* virtually is totally my jam, too. I'm part of tons of Facebook groups focused on everything from hobbies to personal growth. These digital spaces help me Expand my Circle, Connect with Amazing Humans, and BE part of their world.

Whether in person or online, every time I Mix And Mingle, I share my Love, Light, Hugs, Smiles, and Positive, HAPPY Vibes!

Now it's your turn to Mix And Mingle!

Step out, reach out, and connect. It's time to do life together—and be the island that hosts the luau.

HAPPY Thoughts

HAPPY HINT #17: REACH OUT AND TOUCH SOMEONE

It's no secret that physical expressions of Love and Joy can significantly boost happiness and overall well-being. Just think of newborns—how vital it is for them to receive skin-to-skin contact from their caregivers. Or consider the emotional toll of social distancing during the COVID-19 pandemic, and how so many of us longed for simple human touch.

With this HAPPY Hint, I encourage you to embrace the idea of embracing others. *And hey, if hugs aren't your thing, no worries!* Handshakes, fist bumps, and high-fives are all on the table. These physical expressions of Joy are in unlimited supply—which means endless opportunities to *Spread the HAPPY.*

I'm a hugger, through and through. I hand out hugs daily. My parents get one when I first see them and another before they go to bed. Friends and family get hugged at the beginning and end of every visit—and sometimes smack dab in the middle, too! I celebrate with hugs, comfort with hugs, and often give them for no particular reason at all. Like I said…I'm a hugger.

And now it's your turn to *Reach Out And Touch Someone*!

What's it going to be—hugs, handshakes, fist bumps, or high-fives?

Whatever you choose, remember this:

You have a limitless supply of physical joy at your fingertips. Share it Freely, Generously, and Often—and watch the HAPPY spread.

HAPPY Thoughts

HAPPY HINT #18: MARINATE IN A MAGICAL MOMENT OF SILENCE

"Speech is silver, but silence is golden."

This timeless proverb rings especially true when it comes to *Spreading the HAPPY*. Words can express Love, Support, Encouragement, Celebration, Excitement, and Delight. But silence can communicate those same feelings—on a completely different level. Simply BEing with someone in a moment of joyful silence creates an indescribable atmosphere of Bliss—a giant *HAPPY*

Bubble.

With this HAPPY Hint, I invite you to *Marinate In A Magical Moment Of Silence.* Take a pause from your busy schedule, embrace the stillness of the present, and simply BE with someone. After a meeting, take a quiet moment to savor the completion of a team project. While tucking your child into bed, silently treasure the moment they share their happiest memory of the day. This HAPPY Hint is all about BEing present with others and cherishing the quiet time shared—no matter how brief.

I regularly embrace this practice during evening walks with my parents. I know I've mentioned this before, but clouds and sunsets completely captivate us. We can spend hours silently watching the shapes shift and the colors change. These shared moments of silence—witnessing the beauty of Mother Nature—are pure Bliss and absolutely Priceless.

Now it's your turn to *Marinate In A Magical Moment Of Silence!*

Who will you share your HAPPY Bubble with?

HAPPY Thoughts

HAPPY HINT #19: REVEL IN RANDOM ACTS OF HAPPINESS

You've probably heard of random acts of kindness. Well, *Random Acts Of Happiness* work the same way. Spontaneous gestures of joy can brighten someone's day and create a ripple effect of happiness.

This HAPPY Hint emphasizes the intention behind how you *Spread the HAPPY*. The goal is randomness—pure, unexpected Joy. But since you're now focusing on it, let's call it planned spontaneity. Let me show you what I mean.

S.H.A.P.E. Cards are one of my original HAPPY creations. They're wallet-sized bundles of joy, with the *S.H.A.P.E.* logo on the front and a Heartfelt, Handwritten message on the back. A pack of *S.H.A.P.E. Cards* includes ten cards—two of each of these cheerful messages:

- **Hugs and Smiles**
- **You Are Awesome**
- **Have a Beautiful Day**
- **Great Job**
- **Thank You**

I always keep a pack of these cards in my purse (that's the planned part). Then, whenever I'm out and feel moved to share one, they're right there—ready to go without a second thought (that's the spontaneity part). *S.H.A.P.E. Cards* let me *Revel In Random Acts Of Happiness.*

Now it's your turn!

How will you plan to spontaneously Spread the HAPPY?

HAPPY Thoughts

HAPPY HINT#20: TELL A FUNNY JOKE OR STORY

They say laughter is the best medicine—and it's one contagious *Happiness Trigger.* When shared, laughter doesn't just boost joy; it multiplies it.

So, what's a fun and lovely way to get those giggles going? How about Telling A Funny Joke Or Story?

This Happy Hint invites you to connect with others through humor. Try out a clever one-liner with your coworkers or classmates. Share a silly moment from earlier in the day with your family.
Whatever you choose, just let the laughter flow—even

if you're the first (or only) one chuckling. Before you know it, someone else will be smiling too.

I embrace this HAPPY Hint by telling jokes—especially puns and dad jokes. There's something about clever wordplay that always makes me grin. And let's be honest, the cheesier the dad joke, the better!

These jokes usually get a reaction from my audience. They'll either laugh with me because the joke is good—or at me because it's so bad. Either way, I count it as a win. I'm *Spreading the HAPPY* through humor—one laugh at a time.

So, what's it going to be—a joke, a funny story, or maybe both? Who will you share your laughter with today?

Whatever you decide, enjoy tickling those funny bones!

HAPPY Thoughts

HAPPY HINT #21: ACKNOWLEDGE AND SAY THANK YOU

Thank You—one of the smallest, most powerful phrases!

In a world of constant DOing, we often overlook the importance of these two little words. This is especially true in business transactions, where the human element can easily get lost. Consumers may see providers of goods and services as just a means to an end—and vice versa. People get reduced to tools, treated more like functions than fellow human BEings, whether consciously or not.

This HAPPY Hint invites you to bring Kindness, Compassion, Love, and Joy into your daily business interactions. Whether you're giving or receiving, take a moment to *Acknowledge and Say Thank You*. This simple act rekindles the human spirit and lifts happiness levels—because people feel Seen, Valued, and Heard.

As a former service provider—organizing support for individuals with disabilities—I fully embraced this HAPPY Hint. Whenever I met a new client, I'd begin by thanking them for choosing to work with me. Starting our time together with a heartfelt *Thank You* —recognizing them as a person, not just a diagnosis—put them at ease and made our interaction more meaningful. More often than not, they'd leave with a smile…or a hug.

As a receiver of goods and services, I often think about cashiers. At grocery stores especially, many are hyper-stressed, overworked, and overwhelmed by the constant flow of customers. And all too often, they feel invisible. I've found that smiling, greeting them by name, and saying those two magic words—*Thank You* —can brighten their whole day.

So how will you incorporate those two magical words into your daily business activities?

However you choose to embrace this HAPPY Hint, you can't go wrong. Whether you're on the giving or receiving end of a transaction, when you *Acknowledge And Say Thank You…*

EVERYBODY WINS.

HAPPY Thoughts

HAPPY HINT #22: GIVE AND RECEIVE THE GIFT OF ASSISTANCE

Giving and receiving are opposite sides of the same coin—the coin of Assistance.

Both sides activate feelings of Joy, Compassion, Gratitude, and Love. Offering support is a kind gesture that gives people a sense of purpose and inner fulfillment. Accepting help often makes life easier, which naturally increases happiness. Together, giving and receiving create a positive atmosphere of Learning, Trust, and Camaraderie. And when all is said and done, these acts of assistance allow people to spend meaningful time with one another—providing golden opportunities to *Spread the HAPPY*.

However, I didn't always feel this way.

I understood the joy that giving assistance could bring. While working in the nonprofit sector, I witnessed countless smiles on the faces of those I served. Volunteering with various organizations also gave me many chances to *Spread the HAPPY* through acts of support.

But as a fiercely independent and driven overachiever, I never once considered the joy that receiving assistance could bring—*to others*. (And given my profession at the time, the irony of that was completely lost on me.)

That is, until my chronic health conditions forced me to become the one receiving help.

After I finally accepted my fabulous neighbor's generous offer of a wheelchair, everything shifted. The smile on his face was one of the biggest I'd ever seen. That simple act—sharing a wheelchair—meant the world to him. It had been purchased for his late wife, who sadly passed before ever using it. By receiving his gift, I unknowingly gave *him* the opportunity to give again—to honor her memory and find healing through helping me.

With this HAPPY Hint, I invite you to embrace both

sides of the coin:

Give And Receive The Gift of Assistance.

Each side holds limitless potential to *Spread the HAPPY*. And when done with an open heart, everyone involved walks away with a little more joy.

HAPPY Thoughts

HAPPY HINT #23: SAVOR THE FLAVOR

Food facilitates connection and creates an environment ripe with opportunities to *Spread the HAPPY*.

From preparation to cleanup—or even just leisurely waiting while someone else cooks—sharing a meal or snack transcends cultural and social boundaries and brings people together. This universal experience fosters Unity, Social Interaction, Bonding, and Celebration—all of which elevate happiness levels.

This HAPPY Hint invites you on a delicious mission

to *Savor The Flavor* with others. Cook your favorite meal and invite your neighbors over for dinner. Ask your youngest child to help bake cookies for tomorrow night's dessert—and sneak a few together before bedtime. Share your bag of potato chips with a coworker or classmate. Take your mom out to her favorite restaurant. There are endless ways to *Savor The Flavor*—you just have to let your tummy be your guide!

One of my favorite ways to *Savor The Flavor* used to be splitting takeout while watching one of my most beloved TV shows—Anthony Bourdain: No Reservations (2005–2012). There was something beautifully poetic about "breaking bread" with friends and family while watching a show about a chef who traveled the world to share meals and connect with local cultures. Everyone involved, even those on screen, was living out this HAPPY Hint.

These days, Birthday Dinners are my favorite food-sharing tradition. When a loved one's special day arrives, we meet at their restaurant of choice. It's the perfect way to celebrate someone in a joyful, relaxed atmosphere—no prep or cleanup required, especially for the Birthday Star!

Now it's your turn, my chefs of cheer!

How will you make this HAPPY Hint most appetizing? Will you share a full meal… or just a snack?

Whatever you choose, remember this:

Savoring The Flavor with others transcends boundaries and opens up limitless opportunities to *Spread the HAPPY*—with your heart full and your tummy leading the way.

HAPPY Thoughts

HAPPY HINT #24: PAY IT FORWARD

Just like *HAPPY Hint #19: Revel in Random Acts of HAPPY*, this HAPPY Hint focuses on the intent behind your action—rather than the act itself.

Paying It Forward is a beautifully indirect way to *Spread the HAPPY*. Instead of repaying the person who showed you kindness, you pass that goodness along to someone else. The gift you give might be connected to the original act—or it might be completely different. It could have monetary value, or none at all. Either way, it's happiness-sharing from a fresh and powerful angle—and I absolutely adore the concept!

My own experiences with *Paying It Forward* have involved a variety of HAPPY gifts.

One year, my mom surprised me by paying for the birthday pedicure I had planned to treat myself to. Later that year, when my aunt came to visit, I returned the love by covering her birthday pedicure. On another occasion, I woke up to the most beautiful and heartfelt Facebook message from a dear "family" member in Nigeria. Overflowing with Love and Gratitude, I paid that joy forward by helping a friend in California (United States) set up a webpage for his upcoming book launch.

Paying It Forward is all about the ripple effect.

No matter the size, shape, or cost of the kindness, you're *Spreading Smiles for Miles*—and beyond. Because once someone *Pays It Forward*, it's like tipping the first in an infinite line of HAPPY dominoes…They just keep going and going.

Now it's your turn!

What kindness have you received lately? How can you pass it on in your own way?

Big or small, silly or heartfelt—start your ripple today, and let the waves of HAPPY flow far and wide.

HAPPY Thoughts

HAPPY HINT #25: ORGANIZE AN OUTING

Outings are fun—because a change in scenery is downright delightful!

They give us a chance to escape the busy-ness of daily life, to Unwind, Relax, and maybe even chase a little Adventure. *And what better way to share that goodness than to Organize An Outing with others?*

With this HAPPY Hint, I invite you to be the mastermind behind a memorable excursion. It can be as simple or fancy as you like, and you can include as many people as your heart desires. Maybe you take your

Bestie on a lakeside picnic at your favorite chill spot. Or perhaps after church, you organize a scavenger hunt for the neighborhood kids. The details are totally up to you—what matters most is that you're planning a joyful little jaunt to be shared with others!

Personally, my favorite outings almost always revolve around food—because let's be real: FOOD IS MY LOVE LANGUAGE.

A few years ago, I planned the second date with my boyfriend. We grabbed some scrumptious snowballs (think snow cones with flair) and headed to the lakefront. We found a cozy bench swing, kicked back, and enjoyed our treats while watching a stunning sunset. It was a perfect mini escape—relaxing, a little adventurous (try not spilling a snowball on a swing!), and delightfully delicious.

And of course, Birthday Dinners are my all-time favorite group outings to plan. I just organized one for myself recently! *The guest list?* My parents, my Nanny (aunt), my boyfriend, and me. We feasted at my favorite Middle Eastern restaurant, Albasha, and wrapped up the night at my parents' house with cake and ice cream.

Food, Family, and Fun—three of my favorite "F" words when it comes to *Organizing An Outing. The result?* A whole lot of laughs and full, happy hearts.

Now it's your turn, my playful planners!

Who's coming with you on your next exciting escapade? Where will your cheerful change of scenery take you and your crew?

Whatever you decide, remember this:

Organizing An Outing is all about BE-ing somewhere—together—where the laughs and smiles flow freely.

* Bonus points if snacks are involved. Extra bonus points if you don't spill them.

HAPPY Thoughts

HAPPY HINT #26: CHOOSE JOY WITH OTHERS

This may be *my* final HAPPY Hint, but it's only the beginning of your limitless HAPPY Hint adventure!

Make a conscious effort to share your HAPPY wherever and whenever possible—WITHOUT compromising YOUR own joy. After all, *A Happier Me Makes a Happier We.*

At first, incorporating this HAPPY Hint might feel a little silly or awkward. You may even doubt your ability to do it. In my experience, the best way to overcome this resistance is to take it slow. Simply start by embracing the desire—*even if it's just the desire*—to *want* to share your happiness with others.

Practicing this HAPPY Hint daily is key. It may seem unnecessary, but without regular reinforcement, it's surprisingly easy to forget. To remember, try placing a sticky note somewhere you'll see it every day or recording a voice memo to play before bed.

I use two daily practices to remind myself to share my HAPPY with others. As part of my wake-up routine—while resting after my stretches and bed exercises—I declare out loud to myself and the Universe: *Today, I choose to be happy and share it!* At night, I reflect in my journal, noting at least one thing I did (or tried to do) to bring a smile to someone's face.

Whenever and however you choose to embrace this HAPPY Hint, own it with confidence!

And remember—repetition is key. Before you know it, *Choosing Joy With Others* will feel as natural as *Choosing Joy For Yourself*...and vice versa.

HAPPY Thoughts

PART 3: BONUS HAPPY

One HAPPY Hint To Bring More Joy To BOTH Yourself And Others

*Note: If For Some Reason You Are Unable To Enjoy This Happy Hint On Your Own, Ask Someone For Support—The More The Merrier!!

HAPPY HINT #53:

Check Out And Join My Free Facebook Group S.H.A.P.E.—Spreading Happiness Across Planet Earth

https://www.facebook.com/groups/spreading.happiness.across.planet.earth/

Founded on August 4, 2021, *S.H.A.P.E.* is a cheerful, caring community of over 1,000 individuals from 57+ countries—joining hands and hearts to spread joy across Facebook land and beyond. It's a place to BE the HAPPY, RECEIVE the HAPPY, GIVE the HAPPY, and SHARE the HAPPY—a space to Connect, Inspire,

Empower, Celebrate, and Have Fun!

This virtual community is my passion project, my heart and soul. Many people who were once strangers are now my global brothers and sisters. Not only has *S.H.A.P.E.* brought me immense joy, but it has also given me a true sense of home.

This Facebook group and its incredible members have stood by me through thick and thin, offering Strength, Hope, and Love during pivotal moments in my life—such as my devastating house fire in September 2021 and various flare-ups of my chronic health issues over the years.

S.H.A.P.E. has quite literally Turned My Frowns Upside Down and Brought Me Smiles for Miles!

SOURCES

Barnes, Autumn. "A Simple Smile Saved This Man's Life." NPR, 30 Apr. 2024, www.npr.org/2024/04/30/1247768882/kindness-stranger-help.

Becker. https://smileymovement.org/news/petting-dogs-found-to-have-enormous-health-benefits.

GlyphoricVibes. "Stevie Wonder - I Just Called to Say I Love You [Lyrics]." YouTube, 17 Aug. 2021, www.youtube.com/watch?v=y4_bsyun2ok.

Henninger, Heather. "Whistle, Hum or Sing to Improve Your Health - Swan Love Holistics." Swan Love Holistics, 20 Apr. 2023, swanloveholistics.com/whistle-hum-or-sing-to-improve-your-health.

Jeffersonc. "A Good Belly Laugh Can Help Your Brain...and Your Belly." *Jefferson Center*, 15 Aug. 2023, www.jcmh.org/a-good-belly-laugh-can-help-your-brain-and-your-belly.

ABOUT THE AUTHOR

Amanda Lindsey--Spreader Of The Happy

Amanda fully embraced the identity of **Spreader of the HAPPY** after experiencing her very own *Happiness Awakening.* At the height of the COVID-19 pandemic, and after many years of living with debilitating chronic health issues, she finally felt connected to people again—through their struggles and their pain. This revelation did not sit well with Amanda and prompted her to seek a new, better, and brighter relationship with the world—resulting in her mission of *Getting into S.H.A.P.E. (Spreading Happiness Across Planet Earth).*

As *Spreader of the HAPPY*, Amanda helps people find

more Joy in life and business by *Getting Into S.H.A.P.E. (Spreading Happiness Across Planet Earth)*. Through her signature 5 C's–Curiosity, Connection, Cooperation, Collaboration, and Celebration–she inspires others to Cultivate Happiness Within and Share It With The World.

A three-time international best-selling author and passionate speaker, Amanda turns frowns upside down and brings smiles for miles through storytelling, online publications, podcasts, summits, and her vibrant Facebook community, **S.H.A.P.E**. She's also the creator of **S.H.A.P.E. Cards**–wallet-sized bundles of joy designed to uplift and inspire.

A fun-loving spirit—full of Life, Laughter, and Love—Amanda is all about hugs and smiles. A supporter, encourager, and avid cheerleader, she believes that when one of us wins—*WE ALL WIN*!

When not *Spreading the HAPPY*, you can find Amanda embracing her own happiness—writing, BEing in nature, dancing to music in her kitchen, trying new foods, traveling to new places, visiting with loved ones, and hula hooping.

Check out Amanda and ALL of her HAPPY Projects:

LinkTree: https://linktr.ee/spreaderofthehappy

www.ingramcontent.com/pod-product-compliance
Lightning Source LLC
Chambersburg PA
CBHW070648160426
43194CB00009B/1621